AF574004

For Josephine -

so very well met, at long
last, at MacDowell -
with admiration*
and love,

Patricia

6/29/81

* not a second martini secret!

THE DOG THAT WAS BARKING YESTERDAY

Patricia Goedicke

THE DOG THAT WAS BARKING YESTERDAY

LHP
1980

ACKNOWLEDGMENTS

The author and publisher wish to acknowledge their gratitude for permission to reprint poems which originally appeared in the following publications:

The American Poetry Review, The Back Door, Cauldron, Celery, The Chariton Review, The Chowder Review, Confrontation, Epoch, The Foothill Quarterly, The Hampden-Sydney Review, Harper's, The Hudson Review, Ironwood, Matrix, The Missouri Review, The Nation, New Letters, The North American Review, Open Places, Poetry Now, Shaman, The Shenandoah Review, The Southern Poetry Review, The Virginia Quarterly Review, and *Waves.*

In addition:

"You Could Pick It Up" appeared in *The American Literary Anthology,* Vol. III (Viking Press, 1970) and in *The Borestone Mountain Poetry Award Volume,* 1969.

"At Every Major Airport", "After The Second Operation", "The Dog Who Comes From Nowhere", and "Where We Are Going" appeared in *The Ardis Anthology Of New American Poetry.*

"Young Men You Are So Beautiful Up There" appeared in *A Geography Of Poets* (Bantam Books, 1979).

"When He's At His Most Brawling" appeared in *Psyche: The Feminine Poetic Consciousness* (Dell Press, 1973).

"The Sun Around Your Eyes" appeared in *The Sound Of A Few Leaves* (Rook Publications, 1977).

"The Serious Merriment Of Women", "Daily The Ocean Between Us", "After The Second Operation", and "On The Night In Question" appeared in *The Treasury Of American Poetry* (Doubleday Publishing Co., 1978).

Publication of this book was made possible in part through a grant from the National Endowment for the Arts, a federal agency.

Printed in the United States of America.

Typesetting, layout & design by Maggie Checkoway Howell.

Library of Congress Cataloging in Publication Data

Goedicke, Patricia, 1931-
The dog that was barking yesterday.
I. Title.
79-93195

ISBN: 0-89924-022-4

Lynx House Press • Box 800 • Amherst, Massachusetts 01002

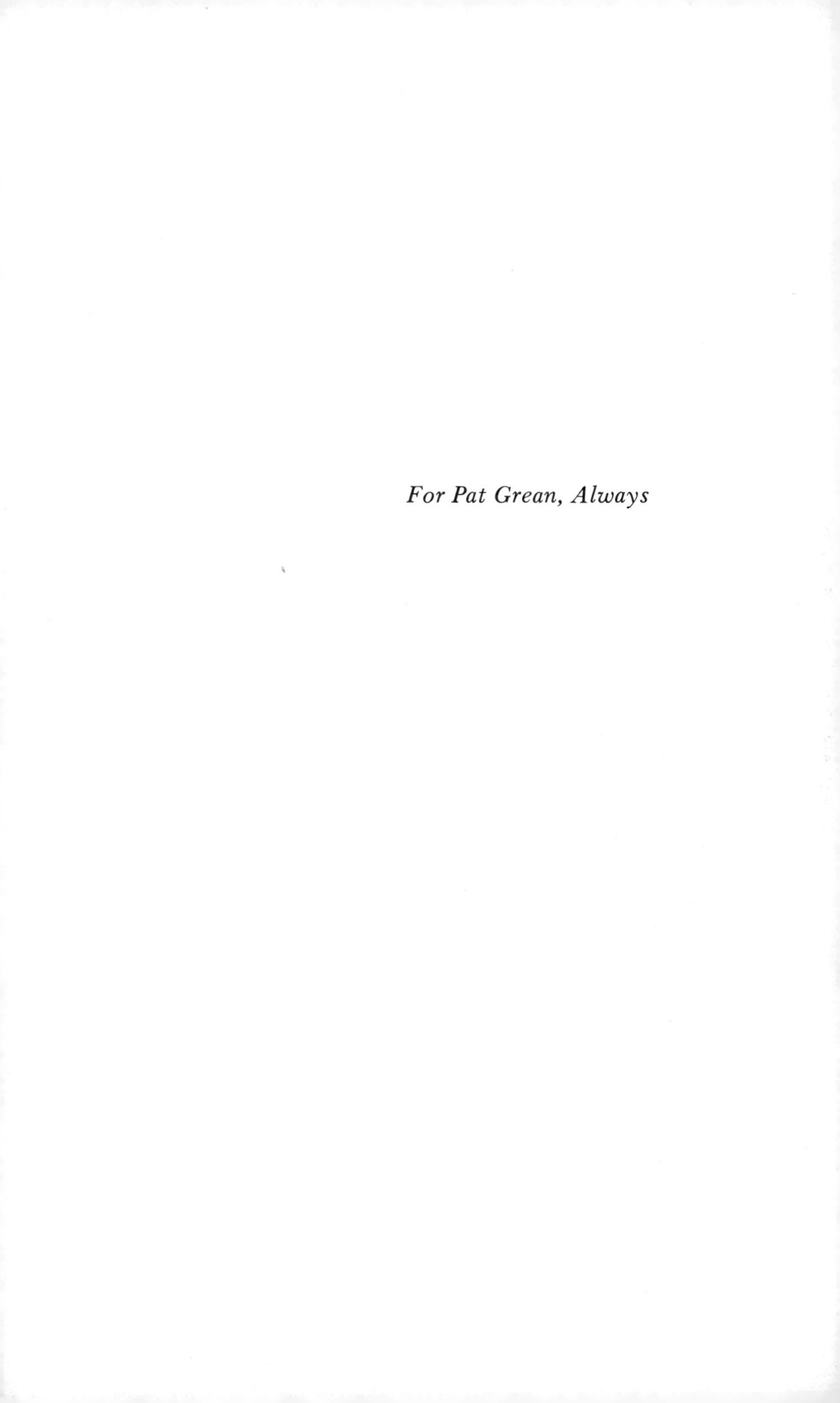

For Pat Grean, Always

THE DOG THAT WAS BARKING YESTERDAY

I. In The Twilight Zone

II. Moving / In One Place

III. TO THE LIGHTHOUSE

In The Twilight Zone

YOU COULD PICK IT UP

You could pick it up by the loose flap of a roof
and all the houses would come up together
in the same pattern attached, inseparable

white cubes, olive trees, flowers
dangling from your hand
a few donkey hooves might stick out

flailing the air for balance,
but the old women would cling like sea urchins
and no children would fall.

even though it is small,
the people are Greek, and it sits
like an oyster in the middle of the Aegean

still it is tough, it reminds you
of wagon trains, prairie schooners
drawn up in circles by night

you could swing it around your head
and still nothing would happen,
it would stay

solid, the white walls
rising up out of the sea
the pillared crown of the temple . . .

for twenty-six hundred years
it has endured everything, but now
we who have forgotten everything,

we whose homes have all gone
to super highways, belt cities, long thin lines
our glittering buses snort into the main square,

the spider web with sticky fingers
glues itself to the town,
slowly it begins to revolve, faster and faster

tighter and tighter it is wound
till the young men cannot stand it,
they pack up and leave town

the sky is full of children
with wild eyes and huge faces
falling to the ground.

O PIONEERS

When you are being brave
It is hard to feel

When you are exhausted

The letdown usually comes
At the end of the journey, the wheels
Stop turning

Sand buckets rust on the beach
Mold gathers in the closets

After 2 thousand 7 hundred miles
In the August heat a dead house

Waits for you, your fat legs
Swell up and the garbage
Disposal won't work

– O Pioneers
(Someone is always saying)

Where have they all gone,
The courage, the stamina, the guts –

Sliding up the driveway
No more the mindless

Exhilarating bulk of the soil,
The pure tug of the muscles:

Just as you're opening the front door
The phone rings, it's the boss
In stale air

Over smooth plastic he tells your husband
You're late, where have you been,

Out of the corner of your eye you catch him
Blurred, red-faced, jittering
Smiling desperately, in one place

Overdue bills like arrows
Pile up on the front lawn,

Delivery vans circle the house, well
CERTAINLY IT'S OKAY

To turn up the air conditioner,
Lie down, take a tranquilizer,

When you are exhausted of course it is hard to feel
Anything real, all of you

Please,
Don't be ashamed.

AT THE DRY CLEANER'S

When first I begin to lay out my clothes
my wife calls me, it's midnight
from the darkened room, I say

"Nothing, I'm laying out my clothes"

and press the crease
along the buttock of the left leg
neat as I can make it

and brush a piece of lint and poke
my finger around the cuff inside

and go on, approaching
the right leg with palms pressed
together, flattening out the cloth,

when the child noisily coughs
I'm annoyed, what if he cries out
but go on

to the jacket,
carefully I drape the shoulders,

pick the lapels clean
of my wife's hair but what's

that! In her sleep she speaks
desperately to the pillow,
nothing of importance but why

won't she shut up, it's all
so ordinary I become frantic,

sweating, a lifetime,
how did I get here,
hissing steam to be free.

IN SPITE OF THE DANGER OF FOREST FIRES

The two women in the car are talking
Passionately.

Both of them are waving cigarettes,
Little tendrils of smoke like snakes
Plume from their nostrils, around their fingers and hair . . .

The inside of the car smells like an old shoe
And the women *feel* as if they were inside an old shoe.

Any red-blooded male would say to them
Think of your children

But their blood is pale,
It is almost dried up,

Neither of them having met
Even one blue-blooded male
In her whole life

What they are talking about is their husbands,
Those wet fires banked, smouldering

Poor noodles looking everywhere for new lives, new comfort,
That is to say, new wives . . .

Are *they* thinking about the children?

In the stale box of the car
The two women worry about everything,

They are much too nervous, they are burning,
Scattered everywhere
In spite of the danger of forest fires

In these waterless townships they go right on
Sucking bitter tobacco
And dry air.

AT THE DENTIST'S

Losing the first pawn is easy
But as to the third, or the fourth . . .

Years later, at the dentist's
The whole chess board tips, jerks
Tilts, as on an airplane,

The tree of your head snaps,
Branches break in two,

Huge boulders shudder and then lurch,
Blood seeps to the surface . . .

The taste of it all night.

In the soft, slimy hollows
Tongue probes like a dog
Prowling the streets of the mind.

Where to? What move next?
Tipped upside down like rusty pails

So dead men fill the skies.

Now bishops, now knights
Now kings and queens and castles litter the land.

This is one life you can't trade
Under your pillow for a wish

But the dentist smiles at you like a Mother,
Through the broken columns of your mouth

Dutifully you cry out
It's only a game, bravely
You insist upon playing another,

In the one dark corner that is left,
Hunched, anonymous, hooded

Before you sits the strangely familiar opponent
Who is faceless, who has no eyes;

Though his jawbone is covered with green mold
His teeth are perfectly beautiful,

Pure, white, flashing
Filled with fool's gold.

FORTY ACRES

and a million or so mules
for customers is all any Superstore
needs, but what else

is there to do? Over the
long weekend when everyone's job stops and the
movies aren't till

tonight, let's go get taken
to the races! Fifty padlocked stalls for checking
out all your pur-

chases, cash registers flush
like toilets flashing and blinking, acne faced
young clerks ride us

down the aisles with bells jingling
the shopping carts, chrome and aluminum dis-
play racks, feed bins

brimming with plastic straw, Oh
are you reined in? Ho, the sickly children cry,
Giddap! Feebly

munching paper meat with fake
toys feverish in their eyes under the listless
vague flattened hooves

of their limp parents wandering
around the barnyard, between the expensive
false fronts what stench

flares their strained nostrils, drains
their gray features, are all those bargain hunters
ashamed? The hunt

used to be only for food
we needed, but now, trapped in these huge Bathrooms,
vast white hygenic

Stables gleaming like kitchens,
even the cleanest tiles are soiled with the waste
piled up, piled up

right next to what we consume,
pieces of cellophane, polyurethane,
all that dingy

shredded yellow packaged
so efficiently what else is there to do
but eat it.

IN THE TWILIGHT ZONE ALL I KNOW IS THE COMMERCIALS

Big things in the wind:
Big dirty things in the wind.

All across America is that OUR underwear
Flapping on the clotheslines are those OUR mangy sheets

WELL I'D LIKE TO KNOW WHOSE THEY ARE

Gleaming like Abraham Lincoln's spectacles
Are those my false teeth

Is that Thomas Jefferson's flying heartache
Do those moth-eaten buffalo belong to me

WELL I'D LIKE TO KNOW WHOSE THEY ARE

Rolling around above me like a baseball
Is that my Babe Ruth, is that MY President
Eavesdropping on the other team's plays,

Is that my scandal with the sincere hair and the babyblue eyes,
Is that my True Confessions, my tape recorder, my
home-made bomb

WELL I'D LIKE TO KNOW WHOSE THEY ARE

If I'm committing the sin of pride please stop me
I MEAN I'M A RESPONSIBLE CITIZEN,

Every four years I vote but I can't help it,
Who can predict what will happen
In the Twilight Zone all I know is the commercials,

But if those aren't my Congressmen or my Senators
If those aren't my brown babies

If those aren't my Jews
Expelled again, from the new Eden

Getting into the same old cattlecars, and wailing
Like tattered black birds across the heavens

WELL I'D LIKE TO KNOW WHOSE THEY ARE

IN KALAMAZOO

In Kalamazoo, which is a joke town
No more

Three times a day
The train whistle rips the sky open
With its teeth

The lassoo of its cry
Howls down Main Street

Like no other sound
In the midwest

It is a wild animal
Writhing

From one quartertone
To the next

It is a madwoman
Keening
The death of her child

How can we tolerate
Such grief
I ask you

In the east it is a single moan
Out of the wet throat
Of a snowstorm

In the west it is a long drawn out
Lonesome

But here it is a shriek
Of outrage

Over the dry cornfields
Brown sheets tearing
Themselves apart

Into the jagged canyon
Of high noon

Clanking from side to side
Of the scale

The long sob abandons itself
Over our heads

Discords slipping
Rattling and railing

It rises like the scream
Of thousands lost

Into the sky like smoke
Over our comfortable houses

Glass may break
Shattering

Bombs forgotten,
Hiroshima
In the heart of America

Large boys
With slow eyes

Listen to it
Dimly

Pain is still asleep
In our lives.

CAPE KENNEDY: THE BOOSTER'S LAMENT

After all the ejaculations
After we leapt up off the earth

Silence

Blazing the black seed
Black parachute flower
Bullet of you and me
Hurtling onward together

Forever
I thought

But even as the burn
Broke out of the engine
You left me behind

Miraculous fiery tail
Fish out of water / air

Torn / toppling
Tumbling over and over

I'm *part* of you, didn't God
Didn't anyone tell you?

I used to taste pure oxygen
I was your mermaid

Married to you, born
Together with you,
Welded
Seamless steel egg –

Where are you going?
Without me how will you swim,

Fireater turned icicle
Bright scales dropping blind

When you return will you see me
Or not see me

Twisting / turning
Joined

To all my silver sister
Half-selves left behind

Flashing in darkness
Or not flashing, dangerous

O Captain take care
You are sowing dragon seed in air

THE BEAUTIFUL BUILDING OF THE PRESENT

I walk to a corner of the beautiful building of the present
Which is white, soft, and low,

Which is all lit up, which is blooming gently, which is
perfumed
But inside it there is something I dislike

And a person comes up to me and leads me slowly away . . .

But this keeps going on all night!
I keep walking to a corner of the building of the present
Humming gaily, in all its illusory excitement

And the same person or someone just like him
Comes up to me and leads me away

Exactly the way it happens at coming out parties,
Also at church weddings, and funerals

Even though all I can see is our two heads, cut off,
Moving steadily past me on a huge silver screen

The person could easily be the principal of my school
Or my mother or my father

Or it could be the minister
Or a new boyfriend or a girlfriend

But really it is my brother, my sister, it is you
My twin soul walking beside me

With absolutely no authority
We are going to try to take ourselves out of all this!

But the sequence keeps repeating itself
Like a stuck record or a trick movie film

For there is no more Malden, Massachusetts
As there is no more Hanover, New Hampshire

Neither for you nor for me, for time, naturally
Has gobbled up everyone's true birthplace

In the beautiful building of the present
Everything real and unreal

Has vanished long ago,
It disappears even as we approach it,
Floating in the thin air of a future

Which refuses to wait for us,
Which will not even *be* there
When we get there.

MISS AMERICA, SOUNDING OFF

Coolbody, delicious in a wheatfield
Last night when you drove me

Like a loaf of bread,
Like milk, like the white bole of a birch

When we arrived, together
On the country road, in New England

Why is it I kept wanting us to leap
Like a laser beam into the future,

Greedy, could not be content with goodness
But kept listening, all night long

Out on the highway to the quickshifters, roverboys, rakes
Ramming their hotrods at the stars?

America, keep your dirty feet on the ground
And OFF my accelerator.

You think I'm big enough for the whole universe
But I don't WANT Mars, Saturn, or even Jupiter, I want YOU,

Speaking like an overheated cylinder
America, you patriotic pimp

It's you keeps making me want more:
You're turning me into an interplanetary whore.

AT EVERY MAJOR AIRPORT

Dear Passengers, I hate to sound reactionary about this,
But even if you believe you really *are* in His hands,
Even if you are able to pray like my husband
(Who also takes sleeping tablets, and drinks)

There's no getting around it, unfortunately
I think you had better be ready to die
When you fly.

The sheer terror of it has been written about often
In poetry, in prose –
Even therapy groups have been formed to combat this fear

But it can't be helped,
Always
At every major airport in the world

First you have to crawl through a caterpillar
Lugging your hand luggage up its guts,
Next through an open gate, a scream
Exhaust tearing at your hair

And then you're in for it:
Thumb closes the door
And you, poor miniature you
Whether you smile nervously at the tiny stewardess
Or cling to the soft pad of the palm

By God you better know it:
That old belly of an earth mother just rolled over,
Stuck up a couple of hands
And caught you, just like that.

Right back in the old coffin, uterus, ice box
There you go again:

Driving an automobile it's easy to get out
Whenever you want to, even a bus or a train stops
Once in awhile, at country crossings

But not here, thousands of miles high,
Nobody stops here,
Even He doesn't stop here
Or, if He does
His intentions are by no means absolutely clear –

Better just lean forward and use the vomit bag
And remember you have nothing to fear but the man

Who, after all, invented this whole business but which one?
The one with the pistol that looks like a Didee doll,
The kind that can pee blood all over the whole cabin

Or the one who, after inventing this next-to-impossible-machine
Of course finds it hard to believe in a God about Whom,
However, there have been several well documented reports:

How, over Lake Pontchartrain, in Louisiana, the pilot said he felt
"As if a huge Hand suddenly grabbed the ship and tossed it up
in the air and then let go"

Whereupon the pilot regained control but there are other
  incidents,
Squawks over the recording device,
It's as if . . . . someone's . . . . got hold of us . . .
Then silence, then the scream of the wind
Picked up after the crash.

Moving/ In One Place

AT THE PARTY

When everyone comes together
Fighting, excited
Each one for all the others,

Men, women, children
Everyone
In one room

Because it is a matter of electricity
Because it is a matter of love
That room will take off into the heavens
And fly.

And whether it goes up and up like a balloon
Losing all its people here, there

Or whether it goes careening from pole to pole like a lost dove
Finally it is bound to bump into a mountain and give
One last performance:

Everyone will be standing up
With his arms around everyone else,

Ribbons of laughter will trail out
Over the tops of the trees,

Animals and skyscrapers will look up
Wondering,

For that room will be golden,
Lit up like a waffle
Throbbing above us like a comet

And always, everywhere
Someone will be waving from the window
Come on up, come on up.

IN MY FATHER'S TOWER

Pickled brains in the cellar!
True:
My father the doctor kept them,

Real ones, human
Quivering like sponges,

Old canteloupe rinds
Floating in a tan crock.

Sneaking my ten year old looks at them
I thought they were someone's lost soul,

I thought brains were everything.

All night, terrified,
I laid my head down in them like an old bathing cap,
I wore them like water wings when I studied math.

The King my father had pickled them and hid them:
I knew how important they were.

Wearing scholastic letters they stalked my dreams,
But billing them as all powerful

As bat droppings, magic fingers,
Dangerous skunk cabbage

I showed them off to my friends,
I swore by them and earned everyone's praise

And then languished for twelve years
In my father's tower
Living on dead brains

Until you came, my athlete
My dear with a dumb kiss

And now farewell to the cellar:

Cabbage head's a flower
Wetter than any mouth,
Dearer than mind to me

And richer, ranker, growing

Like a golden egg from my forehead,
Like a live red soul from my shoulders.

DUST CITY

where we are kissing each other
in a city of telephone poles

where we are kissing each other

in a metal city
a city of electrical plants
and chemical waste paper factories

where we are kissing each other
in a city of dry industrial stink

where it is warm and wet
the round bone of your body
resting on the smooth one of mine

there is a river of dust
there is a live forest
full of enormous frogs and pearls

on the mattress of the iron bed

where we are kissing each other
there is a desert of stars.

THE ATHLETE

Sometimes, when the sun stands up
Right out of the ground

There's no doubt about it,
You're talking to a young man

Sudden as a haystack or a geyser,
Spouting a hatful of gold coins

Some kind of supernatural
Athletic energy fills the air

And you fall back
In astonishment, O
Where is misery, irony, despair?

Brassy, wearing the blue sky
Perched on his head like a bowler

He smiles like James Cagney playing George M. Cohan
Until you can't help staring:

Houses jump for joy,
Trees shine, and the birds with them,
Something takes your breath away

Those rare days when he winks
As if it were all true,
As if there were some hope

After him even old hearts
Bounce in their beds like children,

Like a heavenly beachball he rolls on
Right through town like a trumpet.

THE GIRL IN THE FOREIGN MOVIE

When she walks by – astonishing!
The small globes of her breasts don't fall
They rise, they are as firm as fruit

But better, sweeter, more delicious,
Prancing around in her skin she's a pony
Brushing her teeth, cutting her toenails

Her shaggy mane is a flag of curls
Lifting along her neck . . .

I tell you it is astonishing to see her:
The soft, triangular cunt hair
And the hairs on her head *match,*

Just as if it were perfectly natural
There she is, eating an apple on the screen,

Laughing and then talking
Very seriously, something about politics,

I suppose I should remember what but I forget,
After all those years in hiding

She makes me remember the moon
On the Snake River when I was thirteen,
Naked at midnight, in warm water

She makes me remember violets
And wild sweet strawberries, hidden

On a freckled hillside, in the sun
Among the sparse thighs of the grass

The wonderful tart flavor that was waiting for me
Under the stubby fingers of the leaves.

TURNING. HERSELF. INTO.

Turning herself into a drum.
Turning. Tightening the pegs.

The cowhide of the skin stretches
Loud in the desert sun –

But music she made with you was more than
This march that goes on and on:

Obbligato of the vacuum,
Brisk cadenza of the broom.

The telephone shrills and trumpets
Over and over the chorus

Fiddling below her on the plain,
Opening its mouths like ducks

To receive her milky puddled rain –
Yet in her head this music

Rainbows. Like a violin
The long slender finger

Tremulous, fragile, is purling
Its clear fountaining song

Silver in the sunlight, quietly
Turning. Turning its pure neck like a swan.

ON THE WAGON
For Cam Grey

With the diffidence of a whip
Ill-used, or never
Or only against herself

Her voice is a beehive,
Her skin is made of rice paper
The color of sandy apricots.

Thin as a toothpick or a straw,
Having decided she was Evil

Painfully, at thirteen, she left home,
Then drilled around the world
Picking up whatever she could find,

But behind her whalebone family's back
She developed her own spine:

After hundreds of years on the bottle she stopped
Stone-cold, she climbed out of the mud
Entirely on her own, but now

Everything is too dry
She says to herself, dangerously

The whip coiled in the corner
Twitches secretly, in the dust

She feels like an empty cornhusk
Though she is not, ever:

With spices from the Orient, with red pepper
And salty nasturtiums at the core

She turns herself into a book:
Bitter as black coffee but brilliant,
Scribbled all over with fine print,

Her hair is like dried honey,
Her children are plump as apples

And she broods over them
Like a squirrel

She feeds them rich blonde raisins
From her store.

WHEN HE'S AT HIS MOST BRAWLING

The woman in his belly stirs.
She nudges with her armfuls of blood
The hard walls of his abdomen.
Is it her black eelgrass hair
Terrifies him?
He makes a word to evacuate her,
But she knows a lot of airmail
When she hears it.
The onion skins he flies out to the world,
Full of transparent hostility,
Are not for her.
He thinks he's got her number
But deep in his hunter's body,
Tangled like a harp in his guts
She snuggles in
Like fur.
When he flexes his muscles,
Shoots off his mouth
Or gun, can't he hear her shriek
Under his hobnailed heart?
When he's at his most brawling,
She's at her most brutally gentle
And all over him like a silk tent
Her shimmering laughter
Like iridescent ice-crystals
Shatters the high notes
Of his hysteria.

TOWARDS DELPHI

As babies begin naked, snails
Without shells step

Delicately, dangerously
From one stronghold to the next

Inside the skeleton it is the heart
We cannot do without:

That quivering red bubble
Humming its dim arterial fugues

And pulsing like an oyster:

In the middle of the intricate network,
The contrapuntal underside of strength

Over the ocean beds of the world

The radar we keep listening for
In despair, o my sisters, in despair . . .

Marooned up here in dry air
Surely, we tell each other, surely

There are plenty of them
In the depths

Surely one of them will surface
Somewhere

The waters will turn pale with fear,
There will be a great thrashing but surely

We will know him at once, o my sisters

Finally there will come a man
Who will dare to step outside,

After all these years under cover
Finally he will show himself plain,

Not only the sensitive, pink
Nervous antennae shivering,

But also the vast shining,
The huge head breaking from the water,

The freckled face wreathed
By the foolish horned moon of the smile,
The wily incandescent grin

Of the great glistering dolphin
That will carry us away, at last

Ecstatic, moaning up and down,
Straddling the pearly satin back, dipping
And weaving through the sea,

The dark Apollonian eye that will sail us
Safe home to Delphi.

THE SERIOUS MERRIMENT OF WOMEN

There is a kind of lace laid over the City, a lightness
The airiness of those in love
Not with each other but with their work,

Slow stalking, women with round limbs
Moving easily, at last

Among the black pipestems,
The piston whips of anger,

They have their own necessities, and follow them
Like gliders in the sky, with such clarity

When they have caressed a problem
Just long enough to control it they take off

Over the perpendicular forest of the City I see them
In all their beautiful calm, stretched out
The superior lift of their wings lifts the heart.

SUPER BOWL

But bumping my round breasts
Against your manly chest

Don't be afraid, my sugar
Don't be afraid, my big bruiser

Sprawled beside me on Sundays, lazily
Gobbling popcorn and apples,
Watching the Super Bowl on TV

This may be pretty soft,
Lying here licking our wet lips

And you may be feeling pretty foolish
In between kisses to be watching them,

Those sweaty he-men
Bulling their way over squirming heaps
Of piled up bodies

But I like it too, sometimes
The tight muscles of the buttocks
Hustling it down the field

Neat as an orange, and strong
As a go go girl, or a wrestler . . .

What I mean is, you were right
When you told me football's

Just like dancing, hauling
Grapefruit out of the air
Or walnuts, either way

When you told me, remember
The fresh fruit you hang

Right in front of me, the two red plums
And the big banana, they call it

Inside the plump package,
The athletic pigskin of me

There's a sort of hollow dish
Filled with an eggplant and two grapes

Just like yours butt hidden
Which only means, my honey

The fun of it's carrying the ball
For both of us, when we score together

See us stand up and shout
Like a boy cheerleader and a girl cheerleader
Twenty cherries come tumbling down

So don't be afraid, my sweet potato,
Don't ever be afraid, my ram.

THAT QUIETNESS

That quietness just coming in,
That quietness

Where one lives
Truly

No matter how much love

Given or taken,
All must be abandoned

So that the self may stand
Strong as a mountain, on its own feet

So that the willow may sweep its leaves
Like soothing fingers, in every corner

Behind closed eyes
Pure honey is moving,

The light over the darkroom that says ON,
Don't open the door

Someone's in there
Developing

Though the gurus say it is floating
Miraculous

Like a Chinese fortune cookie paper,
Small warm spot

All I know is the center
I am folded in

MEETING GOODNESS

But meeting Goodness in the street
How sudden!

Fresh as a corncob, a boy
Pitching health in air
Like a wand of sunshine, a reed . . .

Standing there before him with your mouth open
Something you never knew was yours

Long ago forgotten, now wakes up,
Quakes in its slippers like a rabbit

Caught in the act, in broad daylight
Startled, red-faced, stammering.

DAILY THE OCEAN BETWEEN US
(Psalm for my 43rd)

After the first shallows have dropped away
Leaving us gasping for breath

Suddenly the air is much thicker.
I swim in it, almost choking
Except for you

It is as if we had fallen into a blood pudding.

Wave upon wave of it rises,
Slowly the hot heaviness settles . . . .

After 43 years I'm still struggling to get through
These sodden labyrinths that have sprung up

Everywhere around us:
Roots, water snakes, lilies . . .

Surely it is a kind of pleasure, this pain.

In the tender suck of the bayou
Mangroves caress our knees

But also there is this slow,
Powerful, deep pull:

In between rages, red-faced
Here we are, holding hands

Under water there is this current
Flowing like lava between us:

Teaching each other how to breathe
Gradually we move out to the center:
Wrestling together in the dark

At least, for awhile, we don't drown,
We fight side by side,

Each of us embraces the other
With fists or kisses, no matter:

Whenever you shift, I shift
From one stroke to the other,

Daily the ocean between us
Grows deeper but not wider.

THE SUN AROUND YOUR EYES

Out in the back garden
Wild roses break
Over the curls of your hair

Your muscular arm
In a thick sweater lifts

The dog, shining
Black, in a red collar

Into the air around
The sun around your eyes
Yellow nasturtiums flutter

All over the dazed
Blue mountain morning

Between red tongues
White butterflies bubble

Mexican pointsettias
Star the green trees.

MOVING / IN ONE PLACE

What they are whispering, the two goldfish
Suddenly I know is your name.

Pressing their mouths against the glass
Their arms like two shreds of silk,
Orange silk, rippling

Are moving / moving / moving
Only to stay in one place,

The two honey colored bodies,
The tawny transparent tails . . .

In the yellow bell of a streetlight
The spiny petals of the snow fall.

Swept by the fins of night
Everything in the world undulates,

Shimmering,
Magnified by containment

Huge wings
Quivering
Against the glass sides of the bowl,

The golden valves of the soul.

LUCKY
(On June 21, 1976)

By sheer accident having met him,
The man with harvest in his pockets,

With clean new irrigation ditches
And oranges and other fruit trees,

With harrow and fertilizer and honey
And pickaxes and pepper in his eyes

Outside the house I had locked
And barricaded against flood

The land all around it is mine
And rises up to me

Gently, on either side of the river
He has returned it to me

With a sense of balance,
With water under my arms like wings

And even though I capsize often,
Though rocks rake my cheeks,

Though fear rides the center current,
The shape of it shadowy, defined

By dim flashings, foghorns,
The noose tightening around my neck,

Though the life that pretends to float me
Is honeycombed with emptiness, great pits

The first hollowings of the disease
That is sucking everyone's strength away

Because he says so it is easy
Simply to go right on bailing,

Patching up the leaks but hardly noticing,
Sailing along with the wind

Power comes to the right hand
Skill tingles on the left

Relishing even the dangerous rapids
Everything seems brand new

And beautiful, even after forty-five years
All the doors of the house are wide open,
And the river running through it.

ON THE NIGHT IN QUESTION

Under a sky studded with asterisks
And the fat cipher of the moon

First came the upper and lower cases of the cobblestones,
The hyphenated shadows,

Next came the last faint questions of the birds,
The italics of goodbye . . .

Finally the unintelligible exclamations
And loud interjections of the drunks

Past all the living rooms, so late at night
And then silence

Down the long sentences of the streets

The semi-colon of a parked car
The horizontal howls of the dogs

To the dim brackets of a house,
The dark period of a door.

THE STARS FROM THEIR TALL POSTS

And each night the bedroom turns into a cave
At the foot of a giant waterfall.

Even in our sleep we can hear it
Pouring water like the wind

Past the wide open mouth of the cave
To great sheets of moonlight,
The black rock at the entrance

In pure silver drenched,
Quivering, cold, soaring . . .

All night long we keep swimming
In and out of our dreams.

Outside our windows the stars
Are talking to each other, in low voices

But we are too busy to listen,
As if we were children at play

You are a large cloud
Lying beside me, every once in a while
Pricked by faint sparks of lightning

While I climb aloft, in the rigging
Strong as a seagull I grow wings . . .

Waking, I hear you snoring,
Huddled beside me as usual

But sleeping once more, on the dazzled ocean of the bed
Do I ask for you? Do you dream
For one moment of me?

As if the room were a boat,
As if we were blind sailors
Now everything disappears,

Adrift on a sea of miracles
The buoys that mark our passage,
The fires that shoot across the water

Now everything is cut loose
Wherever we go we will forget
Most of it by morning

But here, on the lap of night
It is impossible to go too far
Or too much alone:

The waterfall world rushes on
But the stars from their tall posts are watching,

In the dark cave of the bedroom, somehow
Something returns us to the harbor
Safely, just before dawn.

To The Lighthouse

WHAT SIGN

What Sign do you live under
Is it the Sign of Worry
Or the Sign of the White Birds

The endless tic tic of crickets
Frets itself in the scrub forest
Outside the house: inside

Small no-color spiders
Leap back and forth like pin heads

Over the convulsed countries
Of the violent map of the brain

Flicking in and out of your head they won't stop
Tomorrow's a long time away

Chewed from the dull wood of the soul
There is a fine dust on the floor

But standing here with me
Is such dangerous footprints

What Sign do we live under

Why don't we ever look
Outside our own windows

Instead of poking at ourselves all day
Nibbled by invisible insects

It is easy enough to see them

The strangers who arrived here yesterday
Silent as clouds they sailed in
Like kings conquering a new territory

Dazzling our meager landscape, enormous
As polar bears in mid-air

They took over all the fir trees
By the side of our shallow lake

Six egrets like winged icebergs
White rooftops flashing

Craning their long necks
Against the dawn sky

On feathered hinges they kept singing
Something without words, miraculous

If we could only hear it
Over the gray crickets and the spiders

What Sign do you live under
Is it the Sign of Worry
Or the Sign of the White Birds

AFTER THE SECOND OPERATION

A little nearer, this time
Fragile as clear glass but singing

It is like being your own target
Balanced on a tightrope, trembling

It is the shape of something
Without shape: Joy

Coming and going like heat lightning,
Flashing across the sky.

Leaving the hospital, for awhile
The whole landscape erupts

Into pure ecstacy: cliffs, crags
Sheer drops of delight,
Sudden peaks of pain . . .

I tell you it is ridiculous
Standing here on one foot

Half the time off balance,
Most of the time blinded
By tears like diamonds in the eyes

But after the long flatness, the plains
And deserts of daily life

It is as if the soul
Were stretching itself, and flying

For now nothing is ordinary: each step
Newness pierces the heart,

The tender horizon of the body tilts
Up one side of the mountain and down the other

For now everything is as it should be, everyday
Danger brandishes its spear
So beautifully, along the way

All around you you can feel it
Glancing off you like the light
That hovers but will not stay.

LOST

Miles from here, in the mountains
There is no sound but snowfall.

The wind rubs itself against the trees
Under its breath

If a crow calls it is nothing,
If a branch breaks it is nothing.

The birches look at themselves in the water,
The long white poles of their bodies waver

And bend a little,
The yellow leaves of their hair

Like pieces of far off stars come falling,
Hissing onto the lake

That is smooth as pewter, that is clear
And tranquil as an eye

Lost up here in the mountains
As if someone had dropped it, but no

The pebbles beneath the surface
Have no nerves, they are calm

If a fish leaps it is nothing
Surrounded by moss and blueberries

Flowers breathe among the rocks
So quietly you forget everything

Up here on the crusty grass
The bushes sparkle with ice

And no footprints anywhere,
If a twig snaps it is nothing

For nothing matters, once you have lost it
Down here in the valleys among the people

The sidewalks are full of holes,
Faint memories of far off lakes

Up there in the mountains,
In the great evergreen forests

If a woodchuck whirrs it is nothing,
If a bluejay shrieks it is nothing,

Pine needles slip from the trees, silently
They pile up on the ground.

WARDROBE

But each time she stood there waving after us
In a torn bathrobe, in the front door

Each time pinpoints itself deeper
And deeper

The nightmare eyes following after us
Until we were out of sight, hungrily

Clutching at the last possible air of us
Like pure oxygen, like salvation . . .

Closets full of old clothes.
Twisting in darkness, the loose fabrics sift

And resift themselves
Bodiless, looking for their shapes . . .

Ever since then I have watched them growing,
Endlessly ahead of me I see emptiness

In every lifted arm,
The sleeve of every gesture

Fathers on the front lawn, friends
On every street corner saying goodbye

For the last time, myself
I can't stand it,

What is there left to lose? Love
Shivers in the whirlwind,

The gauze garments of joy
Are shredding themselves to pieces . . .

Shrieking with pain I turn to you,
I wave

Over and over I see everyone stripped, naked
The last bandage torn away.

THE DOG THAT WAS BARKING YESTERDAY

The dog that was barking yesterday
Is still barking today.

Over and over his yap
Repeats itself, the nerves snap
And stretch and snap again . . .

Chewing the skin around my nails
I think of my friend, who is dying.

For his sake I will go on
I tell myself,

But this is my manger.

In the sudden fall of fright
Black as a hood, and smothering

Something hairy and shapeless
Puts its cold paw on me.

Dozing on a dirty blanket
Like a sick animal, like a sloven
I have stuffed up my ears with silence

But Death has me on a leash,
Stares up at me from a footprint.

Forget it, forget it, forget it
I say

Or let me bite down hard,
Let me strain against the choke collar.

If I could catch up with him I'd eat Death,
I'd go hunting with him all over the mountain,
I'd take him to the races,

But drifting ahead of me like a lost scent
My friend's face is my own:

Looking down over the foothills
And the evening plains and the darkness
Rising like the slow waters of a bath

I hear the faint cry of the bloodhounds
Far below me on the path.

WHERE WE ARE GOING

For where we are going the sky clears
Wider and bluer than heaven but not present, not present
To our breaking ears

Though the sweat of our bodies sweetens
And the odor of our genitals is like dried apples

Where we are going our joints cry out
Every morning in a different voice,

Friends vanish, in the cold
Where we are going our arms
Gradually empty themselves to the wind,

Where we are going our footsteps disappear
Shrouded in foghorns, like fingers smothering
The brittle moss of our veins

Where we are going, on the path
To a cobwebbed attic, a dissolving
Far ahead of us like a fisherman's net

Like a foreign tongue, like a piece of bread
We are eaten, we are full of holes.

YOUNG MEN YOU ARE SO BEAUTIFUL UP THERE

Young men on the roof watching the stars,
Young men your silhouettes are like tall bears
Standing against the night sky.

Young men leaning on the railing / eagerly
Watching the fire balloons you have sent up sail away

Into the heavens like burning pumpkins,
Eagles bearing messages in golden bottles,

Young men you are so beautiful up there
What if one of your fire balloons

Should pass through the open belfry of a church
And sail on, into the desert beyond?

Instead of blazing / in a bush
What if you should incinerate a small hut
A farmhouse, maybe even the whole world . . .

What if one of your fire balloons should land
On the heart of the wife who is sleeping below you

Dreaming of you, turning and turning
So that she rises up

Like paper, all aflame
Passionately shaking herself into ashes . . .

Young men you are so beautiful up there
Surely you must understand
Nobody can stop them, the fire balloons

Once they have sailed away
They will keep on going and going

Over the heads of a few farmers watching for satellites,
Over the body of your dead mother

Who is sleeping below you,
Who is breathing the heaviness of lead,

Who is waiting and waiting for you to come down
Out of the heavens into her arms.

THE DOG WHO COMES FROM NOWHERE

Pressed between the flat sides of the buildings
Like a button under a steam iron she's tough,
Absorbed in her own thoughts

She strolls down the street
Under the noon sun but she's not bothered
There's a humming in her head

That is pure efficiency, she thinks
At last she's arrived, after all the dirty tricks

Who cares about the wrinkles,
The loose threads on her dress?

The buildings are beginning to lean
Together, over her head

But she refuses to notice, like a wooden doll
With straw-colored, graying hair

She pulls on her Camel and strides along,
She hardly even notices the mad dog

Who comes from nowhere,
Who does not even live on her street

Until he is upon her,
He walks by like a stranger and then turns

Suddenly he takes a chunk out of the scrawny hand
The calluses swell up, the liver spots spread
Faster and faster because this is Mexico,

The only place in the world she could come to,
Having buried her heart in Colorado

Along with her husband and no money
On top of everything now this:

The long series of shots stretching ahead
In accident's mean jaws

The small carton of herself ripped open,
The one she wrapped so neatly

Torn apart, shredded
Pieces of paper like sawdust

Traveler's certificates, licenses
Even wedding pictures smashed, scattered, bleeding
All over the main street.

GOODBYE

I suppose you are going away from us
Sister, I suppose you are going away

Without visiting,
Without bending to say goodbye.

I brought you up from a small cabbage,
Is it my fault
You used to love to climb trees?

Mother is waiting for us, they say
Mother is waiting for us, they say
In the snowfields of the sky –

I used to stand between you and Father,
I told you what he was saying

But now he stands between me and daylight

Sister, sailing away from us
Faster and faster on your white skis

I must tell you, it is my fault
Before you climb too high
It is my fault you never learned to say goodbye.

THE WHITE HORSES

For love is the child we carry
Between the white horses, with their rough shoulders

Trudging along beside them, among them,
The restless flick of their manes

Even when he is squirming
And feverish, often

Even when we'd like to forget him

His tiny body twists,
His fists pummel our bodies

From sunset to dwindling sunset
Over the mountains, how hot

Heavier and heavier he grows
Bending us, breaking us down

But his breath brushes our cheeks
With thyme, with rosemary, with sage

And we must carry him,
On the long march

Between the white horses he is our jib sail

Even when he prods us, with his little arrows
Even when he draws blood

Pretending to be a tall, strong
Passionate man or woman

Still we must carry him, the big baby
Pressing down on our stomachs

For love is the only crying,

With the white horses on either side
Fuming, and rolling their eyes,

With the border so far ahead
Hidden behind clouds

We must bring him there, somehow
We must carry him all the way

Between the terrible hooves
And brief footsteps of our lives.

FREIGHT TRAIN

The freight train lurches to a halt
Each night, in the bedroom, it wakes you up
On a platform of black basalt.

Time was when you could sleep
Easily, most of the night

But now you have been let off
On this cold siding you twist
Slowly, from left to right

For here there is no rest,
Though you turn to the other is it useless:

Stretched out in his pajamas
He's still riding the same train

With all his baggage undone:
Great interesting drifts of it heaped
All over the compartment

As loose as you are locked up:

As if you were wearing a straightjacket
You look about you, in despair:

Here on this stone slab
In this strange country

Everything is awake now,
Everything is perfectly clear

Here, in the middle of nowhere
The light in your head goes on

Hours before dawn

In the final flicker of black
Away in the distance you can just barely see it,

One last fragment of the truth, the tail end of it
Sliding down the track.

IN OUR TIME

Sitting here in the minister's study
In Marblehead, Massachusetts
We are surrounded by seagulls,

The gravestones are all out back,
The white triangles of the sailboats
Clutter up all the windows,

Historic battles are reenacted on every corner
Approaching Logan airport
The shark faced ships slide by

But at least the danger is not imminent,
(I speak of your heart, of my own slow cancer)
Thanks to the new medicines

Whatever we do hardly matters
Except to ourselves, in our time

And this is a vacation,
The sweet fragrance of summer fills the air,
Wild roses spill over picket fences . . .

Since we have been here there have been 3 burials,
Nobody we know, but still

As the Puritan clock ticks
We amble along the shoreline
Aimlessly, picking up loose pebbles,

Laughing, we skip them across the water
Nevertheless we are careful about it
Especially on gray days

There is so much mist here, and history
The sea breezes are full of it.

TO THE LIGHTHOUSE

Whenever I try to imagine her,
That great gawky bird settling and then rising
Nervously, with all that elegance

It is much too painful, I turn my head away.

Goat. And the odor of goat. Chalk
Powders the children's faces.

Out of that nursery the fine hands
Crusted with rings, the fingers
Sorrowful as bone . . .

Reading the biography I found her footprints
And followed them until they were bombed out,
Swallowed up by memoirs, filled with water . . .

It was not she but I
Who turned my head away.

I could not bear it:
Out of the emptiness of the ocean

Over and over the huge Fin
That kept rising, the sleek razor's edge
Slicing across the horizon . . .

But she contained it all:
Obscene familiar,
Dread intimate of the mind,

With scared, luminous eyes
She stared hard at it

And then built her books against it,
Those perilously leaning towers,

Dense slabs of light moving
Moth-like, over the waves of time.

COUNTING THE WAVES
For Stanley & Pat Grean

For letters from friends, and presences, keep appearing
Like cycles of the year

As a great wave draws up, draws in on itself
And then crashes

With all that wealth of water
Coming in

The children in the playground know it,
Holding hands in a ring, with such serious faces

They surge to the center
And then out, and then

With no surprise but delight
In to the center again . . .

At the checkout counter in the supermarket
Someone you thought you'd never

Returns again, from the windy path
That twists along the horizon,

Out in the parking lot we shake hands,
At the Chinese restaurant there are ten of us

Even after fifty years

Sheep graze in the apple orchard
Bombarded by fruit, the sweetness of harvest

As, after every absence
The doorbell rings, surprise

Every moment we live
Here, at the crossroads of the world

(The children know it, but we forget)
Every accident is possible:

Meeting each other, and being met
Suddenly, in the middle of the street

No matter what darkness, what separation
Between the incoming and the long outgoing

Like comets in their courses passing, like wheels
Of fiery coincidence approaching

Though we cannot count on them, still

Far out to sea there's another
Gathering.

Patricia Goedicke was born and raised in New England. She has degrees from Middlebury College and Ohio University, and has worked widely as a teacher and a lecturer. In 1976 she was awarded a National Endowment for the Arts Creative Writing Fellowship. She lives in Mexico with her husband, novelist Leonard Robinson.

Also by Patricia Goedicke:

BETWEEN OCEANS *(Harcourt, Brace & World), 1968*

FOR THE FOUR CORNERS *(Ithaca House), 1976*

THE TRAIL THAT TURNS ON ITSELF *(Ithaca House), 1978*

CROSSING THE SAME RIVER *(UMass Press), 1980*